ARTISTIC INTERIORS

ARTISTIC INTERIORS
SUZANNE LOVELL

Designing with Fine Art Collections

WITH MARC KRISTAL

STEWART, TABORI & CHANG | N

DEDICATION

With humble gratitude, I dedicate this book to the team of
amazing professionals with whom I have the honor of working.

I am indebted to them for their contributions, which have
created the multitude of successes you will see on the
pages of this book. Each photo that follows is a testament to
their innovative brilliance and their diligence. Their dedication
and professional rigor inspire me every day.

And to my generous clients, who trust and believe in the
dreams we inspire.

And perhaps most importantly, to my mother and father,
and the generations before, for their rich heritage of intellectual
pursuit and the love of collection.

A pewter repoussé vessel sits atop a Korean butterfly chest in the entry
of my late client and friend Bruce Abrams, who inspired my business—not
only with this residence, but with his belief in my talent.

CONTENTS

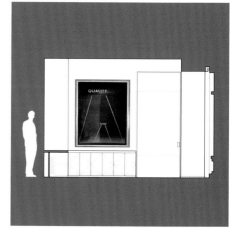

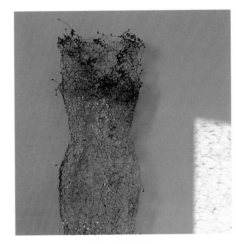

INTRODUCTION

IF YOU WERE TO ASK MOST PEOPLE WHAT, EXACTLY, AN INTERIOR DESIGNER does, they would probably say something about the decoration of homes. That's not entirely inaccurate. But after twenty-five years of practice, my firm has developed a signature working method that is more broadly multidisciplinary—one based on decades of immersion in the study of architecture, the decorative arts, and, not least, art history—and is aimed at producing fully integrated "couture" environments that, above all else, express the special personalities of the individuals for whom we work.

Our interiors derive from three elements. Each serves as a stage for what comes next. Having begun my professional life as an architect at the corporate modernist firm Skidmore, Owings & Merrill, I understand that what's most important in home design is to first create a clear, authoritative architectural foundation—one that, through its consistent language of material, detail, and color, conjures a legible environment that can be quickly, reassuringly understood. On top of this aesthetic legibility, we construct a timeless and elegant interior design scheme in which every space is meant to be used, and there is no moment in which one can't sit down and feel comfortably held. Finally, these interiors serve as the frame for the third and most important component of all: the fine art and collections. By capturing the spirit of the residents, these make a house into a true and genuine home. Indeed, after architecture, our interior design process is about selecting furnishings and textiles, and creating a platform for a fine art message: facilitating where the art will be placed, the ways it will be seen as one travels through each space, and how we will honor both the artists who give the home its special character and the individuals for whom we are designing.

In this Chicago residence, a 1999 collage by Robert Kelly
is held in balance above a c. 1810 Empire writing commode from
Vienna. Accessories lend elegance and scale to the vignette.

As a firm that practices residential interior design, I believe it's our professional responsibility to support our clients' individual expression. Ultimately, each house we create, from its architectural detailing and use of materials through its interior design and embrace of fine art, must work harmoniously to exhibit the passions of the people living within its walls.

The best example I can give of this harmony/love of art collection is my own residence, which is filled with objects and pictures cherished for their history, beauty, and the life experiences associated with them. There are, you might say, three strands in my collector's braid. The first derives from members of my family, who on both sides took American history very seriously. My mother's great-uncle put together such an exceptional cache of objects from the Boston & Sandwich Glass Company that it became the foundation of the Sandwich Glass Museum in Massachusetts. His work inspired me to create my own selection of pressed-glass cup plates, a mix of contemporary reissues and precious Boston & Sandwich originals. The second strand is international: My paternal uncle and his fabulous British wife—I adored her—spent years in Indonesia, acquiring magnificent Asian furniture pieces and objects, many of which I've inherited. My own love of travel has added to this collection—treasured vessels, textiles, and craft works from Egypt, China, Africa, and Vietnam. The third strand comes from my deep and wide-ranging interest in modern and contemporary fine art. I have aquired artworks by Vik Muniz, Robert Polidori, Kiki Smith, Greg Stone, and Nicolas Carone, and objects by Kate Malone, Ruth Duckworth, Paul Chaleff, Ani Kasten, Rupert Spira, and many, many others.

We spent a great deal of time developing the furniture plan for my house. This planning stage is typical of my firm's deliberative process. Once the architectural framework was in place, I decided where to locate all the paintings, objects, and antiques, and determined how they might work together to create powerful vignettes in every room. Everything else flowed from there. The contents of my home, and the ways in which I've chosen to combine and arrange its elements, say much about who I am.

Creating "artistic interiors" is all about the special pleasure of getting to know one's clients and devising residences for them that are, in effect, portraits. In the twelve projects that follow, we have created well-decorated and occasionally quite glamorous spaces. In every case, the décor serves as a stage for the art, whether it's a superlative collection of paintings or photographs,

Architectural materials such as stone and bronze are selected simultaneously
with textiles and furniture finishes, providing aesthetic balance.

striking examples of craft, or unique furniture pieces executed by masters old and new. In every
case, the art supports a portrait of our clients—how they see themselves and their life interests.

But good design doesn't mean everything has to be perfect. We don't want velvet ropes
placed around precious objects. I don't believe in artificial or imposed notions of "good taste,"
which are never a part of a true and livable home. A successful interior is one that honors the
interests and desires of its inhabitants. It is a personal vision, as educated as one wishes, rendered
in the medium of interior design. When I began work on my own residence, I allowed my design
to include whatever it was that brought joy to me every day. That's what I tell my clients: If
something gives you pleasure, feel free to enjoy it—and we will work to create the best
professional expression of that pleasure in your home.

WHERE THE BUFFALO ROAM

"The past will blend with the
present to create a future that will
endure in strength and beauty."
—CARL SANDBERG

SOMETIMES A PROJECT HAS SO MANY POSITIVE ELEMENTS ALREADY in place that it can be hard to imagine one's own contribution. A grand Victorian-style residence on Chicago's North Side was this kind of project. The home's front facade and certain of its interior elements were of sufficient importance to warrant landmark status. The owners, an exceptionally gracious and elegant couple, had acquired an extensive, museum-quality collection of Native American objects and artifacts, including supporting artworks and photography—notably a remarkable selection of Edward S. Curtis's Indian portraits.

And yet, when I first met the pair, they had very little of the work on display and, in fact, didn't request that we showcase it as part of their new interior. Their reluctance to display their art said much about their intelligence and sensibility. The more we got to know them, however, the more we realized that if we properly presented it and supported the work with careful architectural planning and appropriate furnishings, their art could form the heart of the modern yet approachable home my clients desired. A home that could both honor their knowledge and reflect their personal warmth and unforced elegance.

Working with the Chicago architecture firm Wheeler Kearns, we addressed the couple's desire for formal first-floor public spaces, all of which they could use for entertaining. Within the home's traditional shell, we applied modernist space planning techniques. We completely gutted the interior (except for the two landmark fireplaces) and created a flexible new program using freestanding elements that "softly" defined areas of use without touching the walls or ceiling.

These efforts proceeded hand-in-glove with the challenge of displaying the abundance of Native American treasures. The clearest example of this integration can be found in a sixteen-foot-long (5-meter-long), double-sided case one encounters immediately upon entering.

One of three bronze niches, set in the display cabinet that defines the foyer, displays a Native American pot and offers a peek at the house's dining room/library on the cabinet's other side. The 2006 oil on linen *Egret and White Bowl* is by David Kroll.

In the foyer, a camel-hair rug introduces the house's geometry. Goatskin panels are integrated into the display cabinet, which features three bronze openings, each of which displays a rare Native American vessel; opposite, a slender bronze shelf extends from a highly polished Venetian plaster wall, against which we hung a pair of colorful tent bags from a bronze picture rail. Farther in, the chair beside the beaded jacket in the stair hall is a beautifully inlaid antique by Carlo Bugatti, c. 1900. The low wall, held back to reveal a glimpse of the stair, is characteristic of the main-floor architecture, in which rooms are gently divided by freestanding volumes that—thanks to the continuous ceiling—make the space feel much larger.

16

PREVIOUS PAGES AND ABOVE: The pattern in the living room rug was abstracted from the inlay of walnut, metal, and ivory in the 1890 Bugatti table. OPPOSITE: Even as a showcase of Native Americana, much of the house is surprisingly modern. A Gene Summers bronze table, above which hangs a pair of classic images by André Kertész, anchors a sitting area in the dining room. The chairs, by Louis Sognot, echo the geometry of the table.

On one side, the case's goatskin-finished paneling plays off of the Venetian plaster wall opposite, defining the entry hall. The goatskin is inset with bronze-lined niches displaying magnificent ceramic vessels, establishing the intellectual rigor with which the collection had been gathered. The other side of the case encloses a dining area that is designed to be as enjoyable for a small gathering as for a party of sixteen people. On this side, the niches expand to become an architectural element formed entirely from warm bronze boxes that serve as both art display and library, creating an environment formally elegant enough to support an intimate dinner or a grand occasion. On both sides, the message is conveyed in a consistent language of both detailing and material selection, which together form a platform for fine art.

While modernist architecture served the design's purposes, we wanted to avoid an interior that felt in any way frosty or corporate. We chose a warm material palette that supported the

Set into a niche on the hallway side of the bar (the beaded jacket in
the opposite photograph is facing it precisely) is a black-and-white
vessel, one of the rarest and most beautiful objects in the collection.
The historic mantelpiece (partially visible above) in the dining room is
one of two in the house that have landmark status.

art collection—goatskin, bronze, and American elm, as well as walnut flooring. It would have been easy to work with vertical-grain paneling; but, as many of the blankets on display featured horizontal stripes, the elm was set so that the wood grain's direction supported that of the objects (and helped the wood panels to feel less commercial).

Though pairing a Native American collection with early-twentieth-century French furniture might seem counterintuitive, selecting objects with a complementary geometry enabled us to make the connection. Our most significant gesture was the introduction of two superb examples of Carlo Bugatti's boldly graphic furniture designs: a marvelously ornate side chair in the entry foyer and a living room side table with not only a goatskin insert on top, but a repeating pattern executed in ebony-and-ivory inlay that was remarkably sympathetic to the collection—so much so that we took it as inspiration for the design of the living room's silk-and-wool tone-on-tone carpets.

THE IMPORTANCE OF PLANNING to our work—listening to clients, understanding how they live, and ensuring that the design supports this understanding—continues in the house's private quarters. Whereas downstairs the emphasis is on openness, on the second floor we found ways to keep the open plan while also allowing limited access to the master suite. Doors at either end allow the couple to open or close their domain to the entire floor, and to bathe and dress without disturbing one who might still be sleeping.

It is a big house, yet one of my favorite moments is one of the smallest: the ground-floor powder room, the walls of which we completely covered with bronze-framed Edward Curtis gravures, which are visible from the street. Curtis was commissioned by J. P. Morgan to sympathetically document the Native American people so as to make them less alien to Victorian sensibilities—an idea restated in contemporary terms as the photos' subjects meet the eyes of approaching visitors. The moment, which uses art to elegantly bridge past and present, typifies the design: well-edited and tailored, emotionally resonant, and sophisticated in its artistic expression.

The elegant room looking out at the street, with its rows of magnificent Edward S. Curtis gravures, is in fact the house's powder room. In the lower part of the window can be seen the massive piece of stone from which we carved the sink.

The office, with its French deco desk and Native American blanket and masks, reveals the house's unlikely but very effective mix of elements. In the master bedroom, the horizontal stripes on the chair fabric (RIGHT) are a decorative expression of the long, linear nature of the architecture. A Calder hangs by the door. We commissioned the Andrea Wasserman artworks, ink reliefs imprinted with carefully gilded leaves, that flank the bed.

In the kitchen, a brushed-
stainless-steel corner forms a
very contemporary moment
in the flow of the horizontally
banded American elm. This
moment evolved from our desire
to create blocks of color rather
than multiple material changes.
It offers a consistent palette
that also gives the eye a place
to rest. The chestnut cabinetry
cantilevers dramatically over the
granite countertop to create
storage without visually closing
off the kitchen.

28

CREATING ELEGANCE WITHIN THE CONTEXT OF MODERN DESIGN TRULY does come down to a thoughtful, and very thorough, consideration of detail. The reason is simple: Contemporary architecture has stripped away much of the decorative frosting typically associated with historic design styles. If we don't put something in its place, we'll have nothing left but a cold, white box.

And yet the details one adds to these pared-down spaces have to be carefully chosen and crafted, as the idea is to enrich rooms without making them seem fussy. Thus, in this house, simple lines encircle the cylindrical doorknobs, creating decorative elements that are as much felt as seen. The richly veined stone in the powder room sink has been sculpted to bring forward its material properties. The decorative motif, taken from a historic design and distilled and stylized to its essence, then returns as a repeating element within the overall design scheme.

Clear, sophisticated detailing can work harmoniously with older design elements. Sophistication is timeless, allowing a beautifully designed home to transcend historical periods.

CLOCKWISE FROM TOP LEFT: We created a custom-designed bronze doorknob that appears throughout the house (and the detail repeats at the end of the drapery rods). The carved marble sink in the powder room rests on a steel beam. Gene Summers crafted the andirons. The detail we designed for the dining chairs, executed in ebony and ivory, was inspired by the Bugatti chair.

JAZZ AGE REVIVAL

"The house uses its elements the
way music uses instruments
to make rhythm, color, texture,
proportion and harmony."
—FRANK LLOYD WRIGHT

A SUPERB EXAMPLE OF ART DECO DESIGN, THIS HOME IS IN AN architecturally significant residential building in Chicago. It features high-ceilinged, beautifully proportioned and detailed rooms—notable for their long, tall windows—in what was one of the city's first apartment towers to offer duplexes. And it has an unexpected layout. One enters on the top floor, where the public rooms are situated, and descends to the master suite. We were delighted by the opportunity to work in such a storied place, and with an interesting client—a jazz-loving New Orleans native (Ella Fitzgerald's photo adorns her desk) who is also a successful, high-profile businesswoman. Our task was to enhance the apartment's architectural elements and to evaluate and answer the aesthetic needs of the décor, especially for entertaining.

The apartment's original design language included very tall, thin-framed bronze-and-glass doors that heightened the elegance of the rooms' generous proportions. We repeated that language—in some instances through the use of paint, as with the addition of a dark line to the doorways, beginning at the entry foyer. This repetition strengthened the authority of each portal and created continuity throughout the residence.

To establish balance between the communicating living and dining rooms—the apartment's two great showplace spaces—we anchored the far ends of each, with a pair of French deco wrought-iron gates in the former, and twin antique ikat textile panels in the latter. The living room's predominance of gray cried out for more color, which we delivered with blazing jolts of red in the horsehair upholstery on the chairs and sofa pillows, all of which spoke to the ruby-like glass top of the client's writing desk. The dining room demanded density; we grounded the existing four mirror-topped tables, which can be configured in multiple ways, with richly upholstered walls and an application of warm platinum leaf to the ceiling.

A lyrical bronze by the Chicago sculptor Richard Hunt captures the
light in a corner of this glamorous deco-era duplex apartment.

A pair of 1940s patinaed and gilded wrought-iron French gates in the style of Gilbert Poillerat, purchased at auction, reinforce the long, lean proportions of the architecture (these find an echo in the dining room, in a pair of comparably proportioned antique gold-threaded ikats). The room's strong architecture is further anchored by two classically detailed black lacquer Biedermeier cabinets from Austria. The "columns" formed by the drapery restate the French proportions and help to create a sense of rhythm in the grandly scaled room. These authoritative elements also help to handle the power of the red horsehair-upholstered chairs, glass-topped antique French desk, and throw pillows.

36

WE TRANSFORMED THE PRIVATE QUARTERS into an elegant master suite, upholstering the walls of the bedroom and adjoining dressing room (which had been a corridor) in a soft blue, a delightful color that frames the views of the lake. A dark Biedermeier desk, chinoiserie cabinet, and picture easel add beauty, history, and serenity. The magnificent master bath, with an original porcelain tub and water-themed mosaic floor that would have nicely suited Caesar, inspired the introduction of decorative paint, in the form of wave shapes, on the walls.

We also added to the existing art collection, which included a superb bronze by Richard Hunt. Some of the new works reflect our client's New Orleans heritage and love of jazz. Others, notably the selection of vintage Lee Friedlander photographs in the upstairs hallway, add a layer of graphic vitality to the Jazz Age architecture and glamorous interiors. The outcome is a gracious home in which architecture, design, and art are at once highlighted and held in balance.

ABOVE: Photographs by Lee Friedlander line the hallway leading to the bedroom of my client's daughter. OPPOSITE: The gold-threaded antique ikats flanking the window in the dining room reflect the authority of the wrought-iron gates in the communicating living area. Four individual dining tables can be set in multiple configurations, depending upon the social occasion.

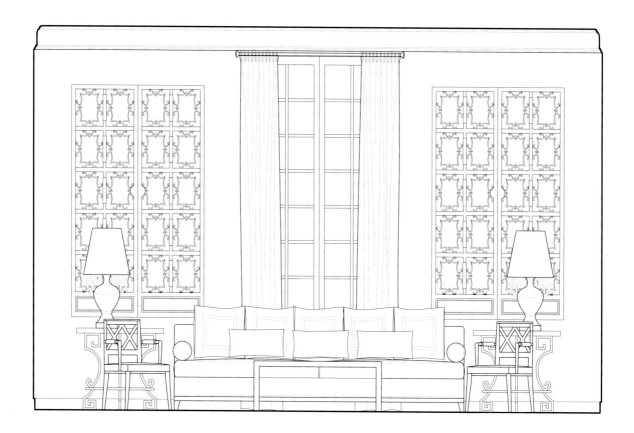

AT THE BEGINNING OF A PROJECT, as we approach a furniture plan for a residence, we highlight those places—walls large and small, niches, points of arrival—where people will rest their eyes. These places will be the ones at which we craft vignettes around works of art: pictures or sculpture, precious craft objects, distinctive furnishings, or any combination thereof.

Having established these moments, we begin to make choices about which pieces will be most effective for each, and how best to combine them. The works we choose to live with are as sincere expressions of self as the clothes we wear. That's why, when we build a collection for someone who doesn't yet have one, we educate with imagery, books, museums, and galleries to enhance the journey. Ultimately, the outcome is a true expression of a client's soul and sensibility.

Bronze frames the goatskin fireplace backdrop; together with the metal frame of the Royère coffee table, these elements amplify the apartment's rectilinear design language. The torchères are by Jacques Grange.

The media room is small but lovely, thanks to the amplitude of the architectural elements. As in the living room, columns of drapery reinforce the preexisting design language. The curly maple paneling is original, but we enriched its color with a wax polish. The richness of the wool drapery, velvet sofa, and wool-and-silk carpet infuse the space with warmth and drama. A regal image by Michael Eastman hangs above the sofa; one of several of the residence's Lee Friedlander photos is propped against a window.

In the master suite, the walls are upholstered in a soothing blue-gray fabric that captures the character of the lake views. Matching mirrors flank the bed. Several images from Aaron Siskind's "Harlem Document" series are among those on the art shelf. OPPOSITE: The dressing closet, off the master bedroom, has its own relaxing window-side perch.

The master bedroom features a sitting area complete with sofa and chairs. Vintage furniture pieces include a beautiful cabinet beneath one of the windows, a chinoiserie armoire (topped with Chinese ginger jars), and a c. 1810 ebonized pearwood Empire writing commode. Having a sitting area in one's bedroom—a place to relax alone, or in which to enjoy the company of close friends—is an especially gracious way to live, and adheres to my belief that every part of one's home can, and should, be comfortably enjoyed.

The bathroom's original porcelain soaking tub and mosaic-covered floor
inspired the decorative painting on the lower part of the walls.

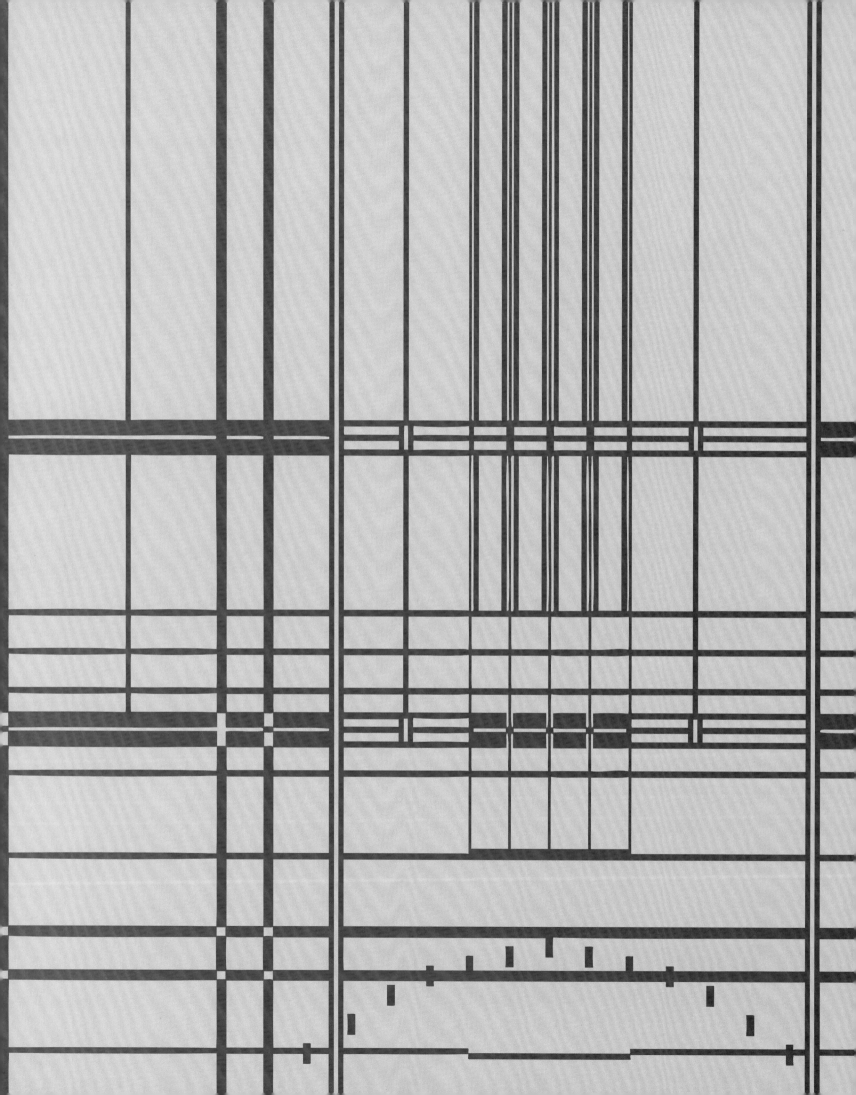

LAKE HOUSE MODERN

"Rooms nevertheless give
evidence of a happiness to which
architecture has made
its distinctive contribution."

—ALAIN DE BOTTON

**Y FAMILIARITY WITH THE OWNER OF THIS HOUSE ON**
Wisconsin's Lake Geneva—the fourth I have worked on with him and his lovely wife—produced one of the most fruitful collaborations of my career. A somewhat formal gentleman with an appreciation of old-school elegance, he had previously summered on the bluff of the lake, in a traditional white clapboard house that—like the couple's grand city apartment—featured interiors designed to look as though they'd been in the family for generations. This time, the goal for their picturesque lakeside property was a contemporary "summer house": the glassy modern residence of his dreams, and a departure from his usual style. But when he requested that the casual interiors he envisioned be overlain with an aura of familial history, I understood that he wanted contemporary rooms that, while fresh and relaxed, still reflected the couple's innate attachment to tradition.

The trust we'd built working on previous architecture, design, and art-selection projects revealed itself when the couple asked me to review the plan for the new house. I knew they wanted glass-walled pavilions connected by fully glazed walkways, to capture the abundant light and views—in effect, a merging of exterior and interior space. But the elevations revealed something closer in spirit to a 1950s ranch house, with low walls and abbreviated windows, because their superb architecture firm, Von Weise Associates, had felt compelled by budgetary constraints to scale down the glazing. However, we were able to collaborate with Von Weise and our mutual client to ensure the inclusion of floor-to-ceiling glass—thus creating that dreamed-of contemporary lake house.

We also worked closely with the architects to formalize the layout, based on our knowledge of how the family enjoyed living. We found ways to erase the distinction between indoor and outdoor spaces, as with the folding, weather-tight glass wall partitions that open the kitchen to

In this house composed of glass pavilions on Wisconsin's Lake Geneva, a simple striped runner leading from the entry foyer to the living room adds warmth and hominess while reinforcing the rectilinear character of the architecture.

PREVIOUS PAGES: The screen porch can be opened to the pool deck in summer and closed off from the kitchen, with weather-tight folding wall partitions, in winter.

RIGHT: The patterns of light and shadow formed by the latticework above this transitional space between the house's indoor and outdoor spaces creates a unique form of ever-changing artwork. The outdoor fabric on the sofa and chairs is the same as that covering the living room furniture, which helps to dissolve the boundary between interior and exterior zones. The blue-gray used in the pillows—and in other of the house's decorative elements—makes an overt connection to the water and exterior bluestone pavers, and completes the "geometry" of color. Beyond the pool, a waterfall created in concert with the landscape architects uses sound to subliminally reinforce the context.

PREVIOUS PAGES: A zebra-skin rug in the foyer conveys a sense of tradition. RIGHT: We worked with the landscape architects, here as elsewhere, to create sightlines that alternate between foliage and clearings and use pavers to draw the eye toward especially pleasing vistas. These sightlines shape special vignettes, particularly when—as they do so sublimely here—landscape and water combine.

the screened-in porch in summer and close it off snugly in the winter months. These screens also open to the pool deck, at a button's touch, to achieve full indoor/outdoor integration.) We also worked with Von Weise to integrate our respective visions seamlessly: When the architects wanted the exterior zinc wrap to come inside and become part of a bookcase, we warmed up that expression with three-inch-thick (8-centimeter-thick) black walnut shelves, which find an echo in the hemlock floorboards reclaimed from an old barn in Georgia. Moments like this one contributed to a grand design in which each element is respected individually.

Creating a contemporary scheme that felt casual and inviting yet connected to a tradition of elegance required a subtle balancing act. The material palette was at once restrained and organic to the architecture; in both the materials and upholstered furnishings, the use of white reinforced the clean contemporary message. Streamlined modernist forms, in the manner of Jean-Michel Frank, appear in furniture slipcovered in an indoor/outdoor fabric; turned wooden bobbin chairs reference a classic New England beach residence, even as blue-and-white cushions make them more casual.

Juxtapositions reinforce the design. The monumental dinner table made of Gascon Blue stone exudes authority; leather director's chairs—campaign furniture—on the table's long sides create an air of relaxation; and the sophisticated gray-blue cowhide head chairs provide a taste of urbanity. The couple enjoys hosting elegant candlelight dinner parties—a reminder of their weekday city life—at their lakeside retreat.

There is very little art in the house—the views fulfill that function. But as we couldn't resist a reference to our clients' vintage Chris-Craft boat, we hung a painting by Philippe Conrad of a Chris-Craft in the bar, visible above a thick slab of wood set with a mix of stainless steel and silver barware. And in the living room, Nicolas Carone's *The Bathers* looks directly at the lake view—as if it had been painted for the spot it occupies.

My clients love the design process and, in fact, are quite good at it—they have excellent taste. It's no surprise that we were able to create an easygoing, contemporary expression of their typically formal, sophisticated lifestyle in this glorious lake house.

The living room is a contemporary space with a slight but distinctive infusion of tradition—white clapboard and stacked bluestone. A foot-high (30.4 cm-high) ledge of bluestone rings the room, terminating on either side of the fireplace. Furniture in the classic style of the early-twentieth-century French designer Jean-Michel Frank is covered in a washable, and very casual, indoor/outdoor fabric; New England–style bobbin chairs and antler trophies might have been in the family for decades. The scale of the floor lamp and telescope (shown on pages 64–65)—both tall enough to form a middle zone between the floor and the tops of fourteen-foot-high (4-meter-high) windows—abstract the trees in the landscape.

In the dining area, three very different sensibilities combine to create a single experience. The director's chairs convey a pleasing casualness, as though the residents had just made camp beside the lake (though the use of leather, rather than the more typical canvas, adds a clubby note). Conversely, the massive Gascon Blue stone table, atop a heavy bronze base, represents our contemporary version of a traditional farm table. And the head chairs—upholstered in an elegantly dyed hide—speak to the sophistication of my clients' weekday urban life.

The layering of spaces—indoor, outdoor, and indoor/outdoor—creates a richness and complexity of experience in what is, architecturally speaking, a very simple house: a series of glass pavilions joined by walkways. Beyond the living room, the enclosed courtyard—which sits within the footprint of the house, surrounded by rooms and circulation paths—makes for an especially pleasurable moment, providing views to different parts of the house, and capturing light, precipitation, birds, and butterflies like a large open-air terrarium. In the living room, reclaimed hemlock stairs, along with the walnut shelves (shown in the photograph on page 63), bronze table base, and woven wool rug, warm up what might have been a chilly, hard-surfaced room.

66

The bar sits at the confluence of two glazed walkways. A long, and very inviting, walnut plank, laid with barware and crystal, it suggests a formal, easy elegance. The mix of sterling silver and stainless steel barware is sharpened by the backdrop, another of the architect's zinc-clad projecting volumes. In this instance we warmed up the zinc with a painting of a classic wood-hulled Chris-Craft, very much like the vintage one my clients keep parked beside the dock.

Like the rest of the house, the master suite's design brings the outdoors inside. The master bath seems nearly as spacious (and just as inviting) as the pool on the other side of the glass. Yet while the eye is drawn to the long view toward the lake, the bedroom can easily become an enclosed cocoon with a tug on the floor-to-ceiling drapes. The room is architecturally very similar to the public areas, with an important difference: The living room's cool bluestone floor here becomes a cozy reclaimed hickory, with a patterned cowhide rug adding an extra layer of warmth.

The ship's cabin–like sleeping loft, which overlooks the children's bedroom and faces the pool, serves as an open invitation to multiple friends. Guests climb a boat ladder to reach the space, which sits some fourteen feet (4 meters) above the ground floor—the perfect nest for a slumber party.

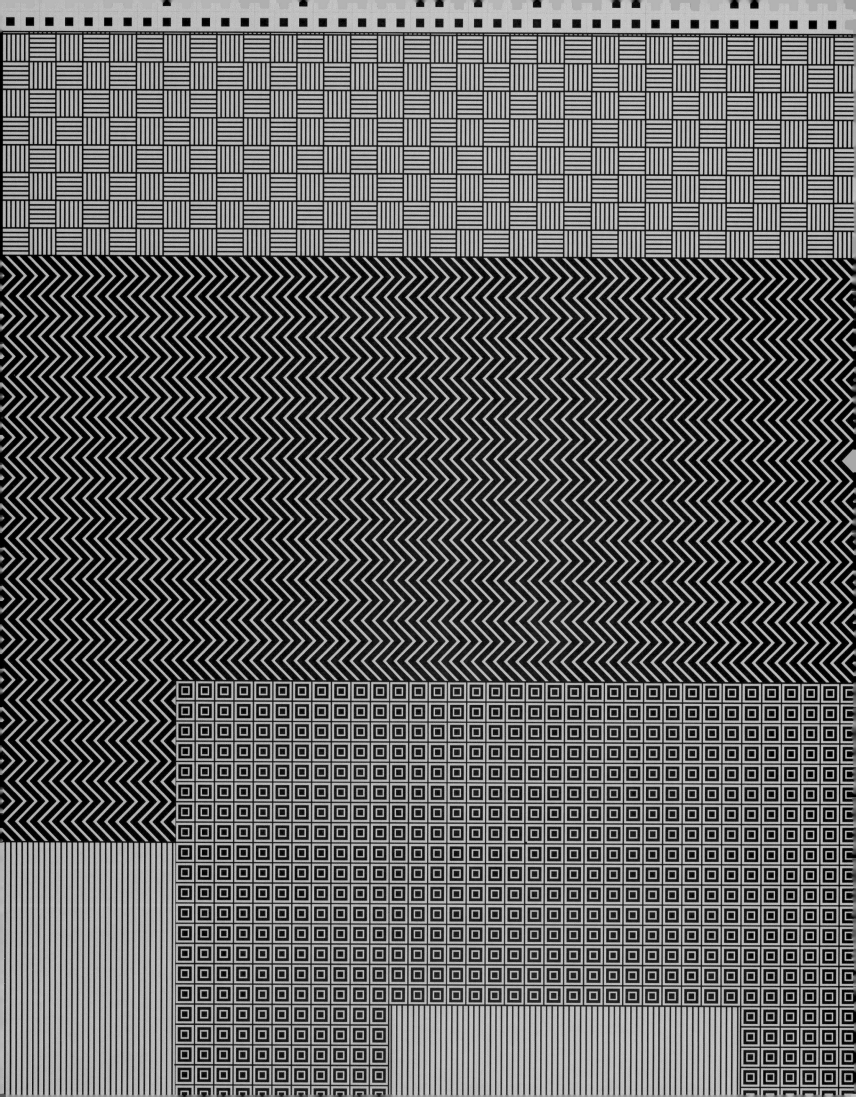

ART OF THE VESSEL

"To affect the quality of the day,
that is the finest of the arts."
—HENRY DAVID THOREAU

BELOVED FORMER HOMES CAN BE A BIT LIKE GREAT EX-PARAMOURS:
One may have moved on, but the memory lingers. Fortunately, new homes can be redesigned to incorporate the physical and emotional memories of the old. Such was the case with a 7,500-square-foot (697-square-meter) high-rise apartment I created for clients in a landmark art deco building in Chicago.

The couple had previously lived in several one-of-a-kind duplexes in the city's Old Town district. Built in the 1920s and 1930s, and revivified some sixty years later by their original designer, these bohemian spaces were realized by the incomparable aesthetic polymath Edgar Miller, who used his skills as a painter, artisan, and master of every medium to produce densely crafted environments detailed with vivid tile work, decorative carving, stained glass, and mural painting. The pair's new home, in a 1927 office building that had been converted into a luxury residential tower, was grandly scaled, urbane in style, and enjoyed splendid lake views. But as individuals, the couple had much in common with their expressive earlier digs. They were concerned that their love of craft and art, their fearlessness about mixing pattern, color, and texture, and their carefree, very un–buttoned-down approach to design might get lost in a sleek, New York–style high-rise.

Fortunately, they had many beautiful things with which to work—especially the pottery and furniture they had collected in response to their delight in Miller's handiwork. Together we were able to create an apartment that, though the bones were very different, manifested their easy, down-to-earth personalities, great aesthetic intelligence, and love of beautifully handcrafted objects.

Changes to the architecture were few but pointed. When we first encountered the rooms, they had white trim and colorful walls. So that the physical space would not compete with the

In the rotunda, which sits at the heart of the residence, a handblown pendant lamp by the contemporary glass artist Alison Berger floats above Kate Malone's 2008 vessel entitled *A Gaudi Snowball Vase*. Both help to establish the craft-based quality of the interiors. The photos, two of four in the space, are by Trine Søndergaard.

Our clients have a relaxed approach to mixing patterns and colors, an open-mindedness that embraces a boldly graphic rug by Bahram Shabahang. Solids anchor the design, notably in the draperies, which form a neutral backdrop for the birdcage and Fran Taubman–designed Branch lamp. Atop the Jim Rose steel coffee table is the collection's most important piece, a stoneware vessel by Richard DeVore. The king's stool before the settle is from Ghana.

Paintings by Joby Baker and Bill Zima (left and right) are propped casually atop the mantelpiece, reflecting the residents' relaxed approach to interior design and their desire to move and change artworks. OPPOSITE: In the family room, the coffee table design is based on an antique Tibetan bed. Again, one of Shabahang's custom carpets vitalizes the room.

artworks and objects, we repainted everything in a single shade, shaping a quiet backdrop in which the architecture's details and lines were rendered in discreet light and shadow. To create communication between the family room and adjoining dining and living spaces, we sliced the doors between them in half, thereby releasing the possibility of a casual influence into the more formal grand design while still maintaining a sense of differentiation. And to transform the very traditional fireplace to suit our very untraditional clients, we built what amounts to a boldly scaled, strongly horizontal architectural craft element: a red slab stone, encased in a tightly tailored bronze surround, with a black, textured "stone tile" fascia.

WITH THE ARCHITECTURE PREPARED to quietly support the collections, I set about selecting (from a substantial existing inventory) the pieces that were the correct expression for this home, and devising beautiful, thoughtfully considered vignettes that combined fine art and objects in surprising ways. Surprise was essential: My clients are spontaneous, flexible people who don't hesitate to change things, and my tableaux—however well-planned—had to maintain that spontaneous spirit. Sometimes we achieved this spirit through juxtapositions, as with the round-headed Matisse above a circular sculpture atop a Le Corbusier chest. Elsewhere, we did just enough to allow things to happen: The thin bronze shelf in the entry, which supports a Bertoia wire sculpture and art nouveau vessels, is an example of this spontaneity of design, as are the black-brown lacquered bedroom nightstands that contain selected ceramics. We also paired objects with similar spirits: hence the bronze Burmese Buddha head atop the Stickley sideboard—from the same period but a very different country—in the dining room. And when we introduced objects/design elements, we maintained the mix of vitality and beauty inherent in the couple's style. This mix is exemplified by four handmade Iranian carpets, exceptional for both the boldness of their designs and incomparable quality of craft. Both are by the modern textile designer and master weaver Bahram Shabahang.

In every particular, character was key: My clients are philanthropic, open-minded individuals who delight in life and all its colors, and their new home expresses that spirit. It may be on a high floor in a chic district, but Edgar Miller would have been pleased.

In the dining room, the commanding painting by Ruprecht von Kaufmann dates from 1974. Two of the Ole Wanscher chairs surrounding my custom-designed lacquer-and-bronze table are original; the others are commissioned copies. The brass chandelier is "after" one in the Galerie Historismus collection.

CLOCKWISE FROM UPPER LEFT: In the entry, a c. 1900 French repoussé mirror. Charles Burchfield's
Sunburst in December above an Arts and Crafts runner. Outside the powder room,
Fontainebleau wallpaper by Jackie Kazarian. A Milton Avery canvas above a knobbed Axel Salto
vessel. OPPOSITE: A Matisse hangs above a cabinet by Le Corbusier and Charlotte Perriand.

For the master bedroom, a custom-crafted overscale nightstand contains selections from my clients' ceramic collection. Works by Milton Avery and David Burliuk (by the lamp) are above. The bed and walls are upholstered in fabrics from my Twill Textiles collection, creating a quiet, intimate cocoon.

GLAMOUR WITH A VOICE

"For it is our business only to make
the best Use we can of the
Powers granted us by Nature, and
whatever we take in Hand,
to do it with all our Might."

—CICERO

THE CREATION OF THIS NEW YORK PIED-À-TERRE REQUIRED THAT WE combine two distinct—and distinctive—personalities into a singular design experience. The first was that of my client, a hardworking and successful entrepreneur who is also a connoisseur of haute couture and possessed of a fabulous sense of style. The second belonged to the space itself: a one-bedroom suite in one of Manhattan's great Beaux-Arts hotels, its rooms distinguished by high ceilings, ideal proportions, and superlative architectural details—the very best of Belle Epoque elegance. The two sensibilities—one of-the-moment, the other Old World—were both the height of chic. We wondered how to alchemize them into something genuinely original.

We began by honoring the architecture in a way that enhanced its details, while also addressing my client's need for a flexible living/working/entertaining environment. The functions of the two principal spaces—living room and bedroom—were reversed to allow the suite's large and formal French window to greet the eye when one entered from the new foyer. A massive, high-gloss, black lacquer portal was placed directly in the center of the wall between the spaces, an axial connection that opened the suite visually from end to end, making it seem larger, more cohesive, and, not least, more grand.

The impeccable original detailing, executed in sculpted plaster, and all of the Beaux-Arts interior architecture—which infused the suite with authority and elegance—were restored and preserved. To them, we added an element of unexpected glamour. Because the space had no views, despite its high floor and close proximity to Central Park, we replaced the existing blank wall panels with a series of back-painted glass eglomise murals, executed in black against an austere storm-cloud blue. These collectively form a fantasy arcadian vista—a shimmering, jewel-like gesture that combines a contemporary graphic style with a historic decorative technique to deliver a vitalizing jolt of modernity.

For this New York City pied-à-terre, we replaced the undistinguished off-center door between the rooms with a dramatic full-height portal at the exact center of the wall, opening the suite from end to end with the drama of black high-gloss lacquer. OVERLEAF: The living room's ornate Indian silver-leaf mirror—on a reflective wall—captures Kara Walker's provocative artwork, hanging in the bedroom. The c. 1808 English klismos chairs feature their original gilt decoration.

KARA WALKER PICTURES FROM ANOTHER TIME

The predominance of pale blue in the color palette—which might have tipped over into sweetness—is given mystery and allure through striking infusions of black, notably in the portal between the rooms, the vintage furniture pieces, and the living room's supremely chic Baccarat chandelier. Reflective silver leaf on the living room wall and crown moldings, custom-designed mirrored nightstands flanking the bed, and gleaming lacquerwork extend and animate the spaces, drawing in the bright lights of the city. Given my client's discerning fashion sense—her appreciation for the well-turned detail—I treated certain elements like couture. The tie-backs for the silk draperies, for example, combine leather and linen, and a strongly architectural weave structure of a python-skin pattern appears on the throw pillows and cushions.

The girl in the painting overlooks the gilt metal French deco table, surrounded by horsehair-upholstered stools—all perched atop a custom-designed carpet featuring a plan of Milan, international capital of fashion and our client's favorite destination. The black glass tabletop finds a spectacular echo directly above, in the rare black Baccarat chandelier.

The turtle sitting on the rock closely observes Greg Lauren's *Girl in a Wedding Dress*—suspended on slender cables from anchors in the millwork. Creating the mural, executed in *verre églomisé*—back-painted glass—involved drawing the views that gave magical depth to the rooms, transferring the drawings to the glass with pen and ink, and finally adding layers of dramatic cloudy blue-gray color.

A provocative and exceptional mural from the artist Kara Walker's "silhouette" series commands a wall in the master bedroom. Its strength provides a powerful juxtaposition to the feminine elegance of the room. Our mirrored bedside tables, and the mercury-glass lamps atop them, enhance the space's glamour. The handwoven bouclé throw, edged in kid suede, and the mink-trimmed pillows capture the suite's overall material sumptuousness. Back-painted black-bevel details on the night tables, and black lines on the lampshades and beneath the molding, bring a muscular architectural presence to a feminine environment.

98

GLAMOUR RESONATES AS WELL IN UNEXPECTED WAYS, notably in the custom-designed woven silk carpet featuring a historic map of Milan, my client's favorite city. We carefully laid out the plan so that the Milanese emblem falls in the foyer, right at the entry.

For all its controlled extravagance, the interior also reflects my client's seriousness and discernment, as expressed in her powerful collection of contemporary art. Kara Walker's white-on-black cut-paper "silhouette" mural, a fictionalized historical narrative of master-and-slave relations in the antebellum South, consumes the primary elevation. This magnificent artwork is as visually playful as it is disturbing, making its commanding presence in the opulent setting all the more provocative.

If the painted glass panels and cartographic carpet surprise with their fantastical glamour, Walker's mural does so with its audacity. Collectively they contribute to a portrait of my client's nature: ultra-stylish, independent-minded, and wise.

OPPOSITE: In the "gentleman's suite," a photograph by Jack Spencer above the chaise and a spectacular woven-leather Hermès throw reinforce the well-tailored, urbane design scheme. A silvered metal floor lamp with handcrafted flexible joints, designed by Eduard-Wilfried Buquet in 1927, is a model of Bauhaus-era functionalist elegance.

The fabric encasing this room with the comfortable snugness of a well-tailored suit was calibrated by the office and woven by Twill Textiles, with the exception of the headboard, which Sam Kasten wove by hand with a thick linen weft to provide strength of character. We used a bouclé yarn on the chaise to give it comfort and texture. High-sheen navy-blue lacquered wainscoting and night tables, and the dark gray-blue lacquered "frame" around the walls, anchor and reinforce the room's architecture. The Jack Spencer photographs are from a series documenting the American South. Vik Muniz's *The Tower of Babel, after Pieter Breugel (Gordian Puzzle)* looms intriguingly above the bed.

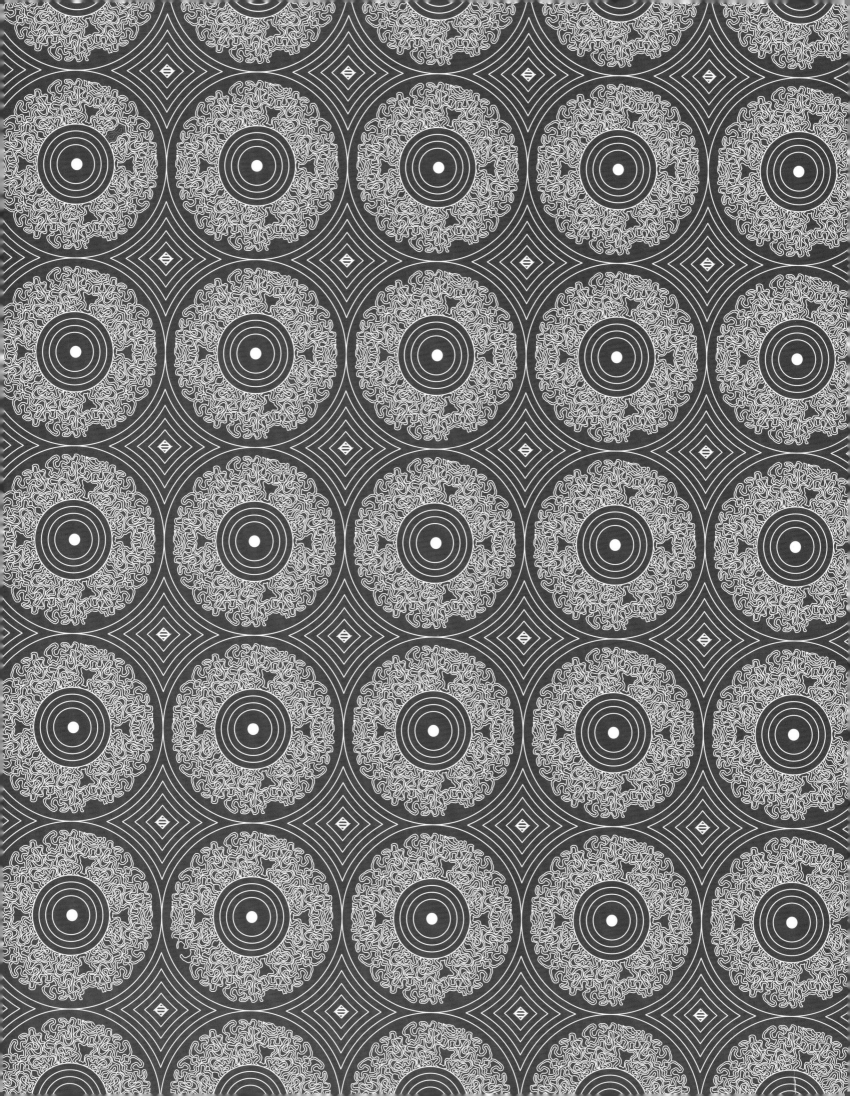

A FEATHERED NEST

"The room is not only the beginning
of architecture: it is an extension of self...
a choosing, conscious individual."
—LOUIS KAHN

W

HEN I FIRST SAW MY HOME, A THREE-STORY TOWN HOUSE across the street from Chicago's Lincoln Park Zoo, its virtues were immediately apparent. They began at the entrance, which was set a floor above street level, as in a Mediterranean hillside villa. One entered through a gate and walked up a private outdoor stair to the front door, a separation that added a layer of security while creating a gracious transition from the urban world outside the gate to the peaceful interior. Inside, rather than the narrow floor plates with square footage–consuming side stairs one typically finds in the city, the four levels were unusually broad and allowed for big, comfortably scaled rooms—dimensions magisterially enhanced by eleven-foot (3.3-meter) ceilings. The front and rear facades captured both eastern and western light. In the middle of the house a circular stair culminated in a skylight, which meant natural illumination everywhere, even in the structure's heart. The house also offered that most precious of city-dwelling luxuries: two terraces overlooking Lincoln Park and a third, off the kitchen, large enough to be enjoyed as an outdoor room.

Redesiging my home was not without challenges. The floors had been divided into a series of small rooms so that one didn't feel their amplitude. The house's moldings, trim, and details were overdone and applied to excess. Colonial-style columns proliferated. But I hadn't the slightest doubt that I could take full advantage of the opportunity the house represented.

I was also sure that this house offered many opportunities to display my art. Over the years, I've built a number of collections drawing on many sources. Putting this house together offered the chance to sift through my collection and honor my favorite things, whether precious or utilitarian, in a comfortable yet elegant environment.

As my own client, I began as we always do: with the architecture. We started by gutting the warren of rooms to create open spaces. On the first, public floor, we converted the dining

A brass monkey by the Mexican artist Sergio Bustamante
swings easily above the entry stairs and ponders a collection
of imported silk ikats—reflected in a silver-leaf mirror.

room to a library and exposed it completely to the adjacent living room. We raised door heights to accentuate the soaring ceilings; and stripped away fussy architectural details, replacing them with simpler elements, such as the circular stair's Shaker-inspired ebonized walnut handrail. We exchanged the narrow floorboards for wider ones in rift-sawn oak, which gave the house a more casual look—but we infused them with a dark finish for an overlay of elegance. Our attention to detail extended even to the solid parapet walls of the terraces, which we replaced with glass. The glass made each of the house's floors seem larger. Looking out, the view extends to the lush greenery of Lincoln Park.

AS FOR FURNISHINGS, I have memory-rich pieces from family members, but our new home afforded an opportunity to add a few new things, notably a rope-wrapped table by the French designer Christian Astuguevieille. Another object I included was a five-foot-square (1.5-meter-square) cast-bronze-and-glass coffee table by Gene Summers. Mies van der Rohe's right-hand man on the Seagram Building, Summers participated in some of the great modern buildings of the twentieth century; his work synthesizes an architectural tradition I deeply respect and my enduring interest in craft.

Edward Lipski's bird, suspended above an Astuguevieille rope table at the edge of the library, seems to thoughtfully consider the Miró on the far side of the living room. The bird and table create a porous separation between the two rooms. The layered furniture successfully makes the whole space seem larger and more complex.

In the library, the cast-bronze-and-glass coffee table by Gene Summers creates a space within a space. On top of it, I placed a large vessel created by Paul Chaleff, and a tea set, a gift from Ani Kasten. The reflectivity of the wall-size silver-leaf mirror, behind Vik Muniz's *After Gerhard Richter* (a portrait of Richter's daughter Betty, who's looking over her shoulder at the view) reveals the winding stairway on the opposite side of the space. The hanging lamps reduce clutter on the tabletops flanking the sofa while opening up the library. The suite of art books on the coffee table includes folios of work by Miró and Calder, beneath a copy of Daniel Burnham's 1909 plan for Chicago.

110

WITH THE ARCHITECTURE in place and the house's contents chosen, I began thinking about vignettes. Moving through a home, one is in a perpetual state of arrival—in rooms, on stair landings, at the transition points between spaces. Each of these represented an opportunity to create a unique moment, one that might juxtapose elements from different parts of my collections in unexpected yet illuminating ways. For example, a contemporary photograph by Robert Polidori hangs alongside a work by Madame Vigée-Lebrun, Marie Antoinette's portraitist, that belonged to a favorite aunt—a juxtaposition that sets a historical artwork to which I have a sentimental attachment within a contemporary aesthetic context.

I also incorporated certain vignettes that I'd worked on in other houses of mine. The 1830 portrait of my ancestor Russell Buckman Lovell, by John Blunt, hangs above a Federal secretary in the entry, with a contemporary porcelain vessel by Paul Chaleff beneath. Among the individually lit etchings climbing the stairwell are ones that once belonged to Frank Lloyd Wright, which were given to my husband's father as payment for legal services. Opportunities presented themselves with delightful unexpectedness: Why not separate the large-scale "sunflower" diptych, by Sally Chandler, so that the panels could speak to each other from across the room rather than side by side? And I optically extended the library space by mirroring one wall and hanging Vik Muniz's *After Gerhard Richter*—a portrait of Richter's daughter Betty looking backward over her shoulder—on the mirror itself, so she appears to be looking into the looking glass.

Slowly but steadily, everything found its place. One of the truths that years of practice has taught me is that an artless simplicity is only achieved after many hours of design studies and thoughtful consideration. For example, I devoted much time to finding a harmonious order that balanced pattern and color in the display of Boston & Sandwich Glass Company cup plates in the entry. Then I chose a dark shade for the wall behind them, as white would have made the objects look too precious. Portraits of my mother's great-uncle and his wife in gilded Victorian frames flank *Prayer*, a contemporary expression of the American flag rendered in tar and paper by the artist Greg Stone. The applied design of a dining tray from Indonesia lives more vividly beside a sculptural Chinese moon-gazing chair in the master bedroom.

The artist Nina Levy's cast-resin "crown of torsos" enlivens a corner of the library.
The contemporary Asian lantern, one of a pair, originally held a candle. We replaced the rice paper with glass and wired the lantern, making it more contemporary.
The armchair is upholstered in an eggplant-and-cream fabric handwoven by Sam Kasten.

Behind the Miró (on a reproduction Jacques-Emile Ruhlmann easel) a Picasso vessel sits atop a tall carved walnut table. Drawings by Whistler and Rubens, left and right, hang above the fireplace. An Indonesian ceremonial food box, atop a Chinese shoe chest and to the right of the Miró, adds to the vignette's strong graphic quality.

Throughout the house, objects are highlighted and vitalized by their unexpected contexts. Ceremonial Chinese food boxes and Kenyan ostrich eggs sit in the living room. A rare textile purchased on a trip to Vietnam hangs in the master closet. Vernacular Indonesian deer heads of carved and painted wood adorn the wall of the gleaming Bulthaup kitchen. A seventeenth-century Burmese Buddha sits behind my twentieth-century industrial-steel desk.

MANY EXQUISITE CRAFT OBJECTS help to personalize the house, in part because of the care with which I selected them, but largely because they introduce each artist's hand into the rooms. And everywhere one looks, there is a diversity of art: graceful (Nicolas Carone's canvas *The Disciple* over a bed); rectilinear (*Geometric Unfolding*, a classic Herbert Bayer graphic painting); whimsical (Constance Roberts's carved wooden handbag, appropriately in the dressing room); serious (Picasso, Miró); iconoclastic (Keysook Geum's pink lotus "web" dress in my daughter's bedroom).

The art collection is a vast and diverse assembly, to be sure. But if one piece sums up my spirit, it is Edward Lipski's six-foot-high (2-meter-high) sculpture of a black bird—covered in actual raven feathers—that hangs above the Astuguevieille table. I selected it because, in concert with the table, the bird enabled me to combine art and design to achieve an architectural objective—that is, the porous separation of two spaces. But I also chose it for a more personal reason: When I asked the dealer Alan Koppel about it, he replied, memorably, "Well, welcome to my cage"—a phrase I now use often.

In the living room, two nineteenth-century portraits of family members flank *Prayer*, an abstraction of four American flags rendered in tar on paper by the contemporary artist Greg Stone. Objects found on my travels include a Burmese Buddha and an elegant pricket candlestick from China. Deco-style armchairs combine long-haired cowhide with a velvet leopard print— a combination I love. FOLLOWING PAGES: LEFT: The chairs and Federal tambor desk sat together in my great-aunt's home; I added the 1830 John Blunt portrait of Russell Buckman Lovell and Paul Chaleff's vessel. RIGHT: A bronze *quan xing* stands before my collection of Boston & Sandwich cup plates in the foyer.

PREVIOUS PAGES: Robert Polidori's photograph of a Vigée-Lebrun portrait is complemented elsewhere in the home by the artist's self-portrait.
ABOVE AND OPPOSITE: My desk, on the top floor, looks out past a terrace to a view of Lincoln Park and the lake beyond it. A silk Indonesian ikat hangs behind Steve McCurry's famous photo *Afghan Girl*. The ceramic on the desk, by the contemporary Japanese master Kato Yasukage, is prized for its sculptural complexity and the beauty of the glaze.

We designed the night tables in the master bedroom to serve multiple functions. At the far ends, away from the bed, we placed lamps (not shown) to illuminate the extremities of the room and expand the space. Closer in, stepping down to bed level, silvered Bauhaus-designed swing-arm lamps facilitate reading. Books at floor level serve as a miniature library. Suspended above is Nicolas Carone's great painting *The Disciple*. Carone, an influential member of the New York School in the 1950s, is a favorite of mine.

Lithographs of maples and birches by Katherine Bowling hang above the bed in my son's room. Tansus serve as night tables. In my daughter's room, over the full-size daybed we had custom-built in China, is a pair of etchings from Vietnam.

ABOVE AND OPPOSITE: In the kitchen/dining area, antique carved-wood trophy heads join a Herbert Bayer canvas. FOLLOWING PAGES: An east-facing *quan xing* keeps watch over the house's spirit from the rear terrace. Trellising, a pergola interwoven with vegetation, and ambient Asian lanterns transform the terrace into an outdoor living area.

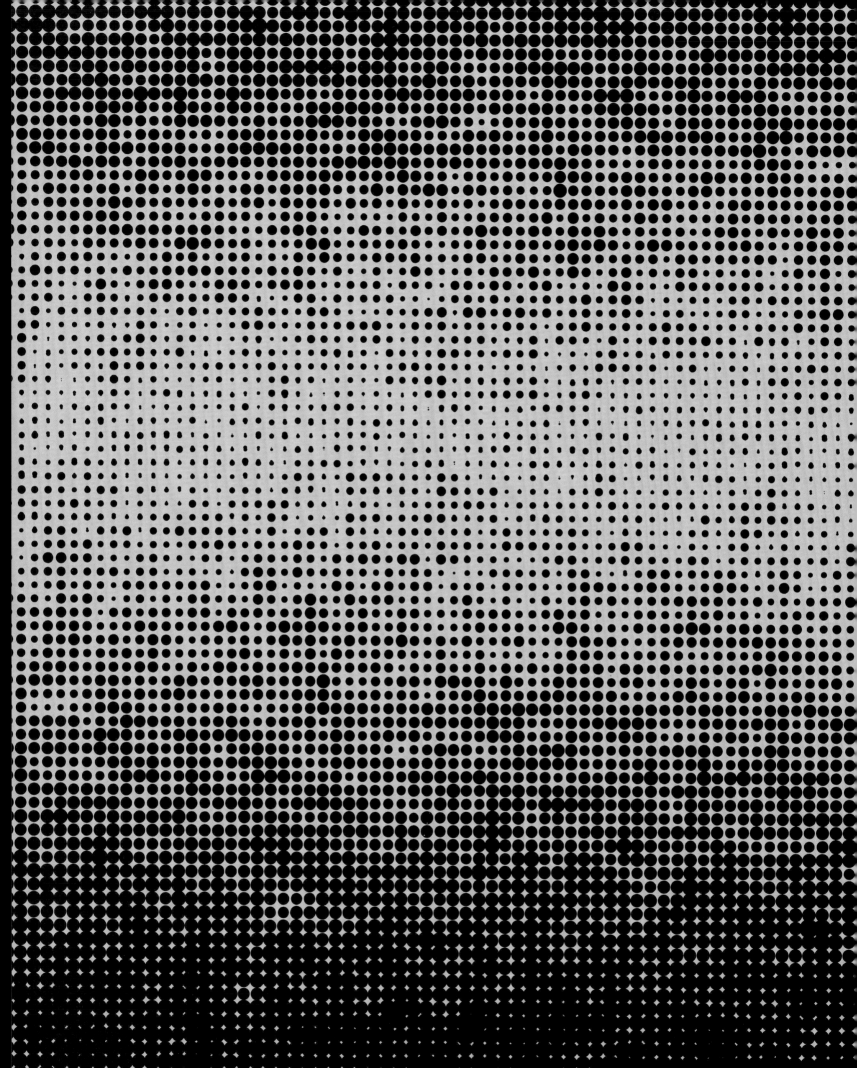

ART OF THE VIEW

"Even the finest artist has no
idea that the block does not itself
constrain beneath the surface;
to release that form is all the
hand can achieve, the hand that is
obedient to the intellect."

—MICHELANGELO

OVER THE COURSE OF TWO DECADES OF PRACTICE, I HAVE OFTEN
helped others begin to build new collections that reflect their taste and sensibilities. I've also worked with many individuals who had already acquired impressive art collections themselves. Here we had the opportunity to work with passionate collectors who treasure their personal intellectual pursuit of art collecting and have developed a significant collection engaged in the conversation of art history. We have always been lucky to work with fabulous clients, and this case was no exception. Their amazing collection is just part of their broad support and promotion of modern, contemporary, and western art—a passion we were honored to share!

For this environment, a pied-à-terre, they asked that we design a space to showcase part of their contemporary art collection, which includes luminaries Mark Bradford, Antony Gormley, Olafur Eliasson, Julie Mehretu, Ed Ruscha, Anselm Kiefer, Yayoi Kusama, Robert Rauschenberg, George Baselitz, James Rosenquist, Joel Shapiro, Jim Dine, Roy Lichtenstein, Tom Wesselmann, Robert Mapplethorpe, Sam Francis, and Donald Judd. At the same time we were charged with the task of highlighting the breathtaking views from an apartment high up in a newly iconic, architecturally significant, contemporary high-rise in Midtown Manhattan.

The apartment in which they proposed to install these masterworks has unobstructed views that stretch from New Jersey to the west, across the Hudson River and all of Central Park to the north, past the Queensboro Bridge to the east, and down the East River all the way to the Atlantic Ocean to the south. The design challenge was that a multitude of small rooms disrupted and obscured this extraordinary panorama.

Our solution was simple—and sweeping. I set a ruler on the plan, on a diagonal that began at the northeastern end of the apartment and terminated at the southwestern end, drew a line, and erased all of the structure between the line and the windows—creating a two-bedroom apartment open in every direction to the mesmerizing vista.

A Joel Shapiro sculpture dances in the
corner of this Manhattan apartment.

Doing this required considerable reconstruction. We concealed all of the apartment's mechanical systems above the entry foyer ceiling. Other ceilings were elevated to their maximum height, and solar shades disappeared into soffits so as not to obstruct the glazing. A full-height eight-foot (2.4-meter) pocket door enabled the library to be opened to the living areas or closed off to become part of the master suite. A simple formula of dark floors that fall away at night, paired with white lacquer millwork, creates the most discreet backdrop for the artwork and views. The custom-designed bed, also white lacquer, typified the minimalist approach to the apartment's objects: It features an impossibly thin footboard—from which rises an even more slender television. The television in the living area is concealed by an automatic cabinet our office designed that becomes a handsome architectural element when open, and is discreet but beautiful when closed, enhancing the clean lines, views, and art.

THE CARPETS, HANDWOVEN OF NATURALLY DYED WOOLS from Iran, are beautiful but also restrained in color so as (like the architecture) not to draw attention away from the art and views. The furniture, which includes Wendell Castle's dark cherry *Lap Dog*, is similarly restrained. A built-in kitchen banquet and minimalist, gray-stone architectural elements that complement the kitchen counters were strategically added to serve as kitchen desk, dining room bar, and entry bench, thus enhancing the clean lines while simultaneously providing interest and practicalities.

Among the many pleasures of the design process, I think I may enjoy the placement of art the most—if properly played, the effect is of a well-orchestrated sequence of expression. These clients are masters at adjacencies and they experiment freely with location and dialogue. The 2009 Antony Gormley sculpture *Standing Matter*, constructed from forged steel ball bearings, is positioned at the end of a long hallway, engaged in dialogue with Donald Judd's 1967 red lacquer on galvanized iron progression *Untitled* at the other end of the apartment. A wall-size Mark Bradford collage is in juxtaposition with a wall-size George Baseliz oil. *Monica*, a languid, piquant nude by Tom Wesselmann, hangs where it should—over the bed.

As a designer I try to partner discreetly with my clients. In this instance it was fun to collaborate on design and an honor to stand back and allow a fantastic fine art collection to take center stage.

Olafur Eliasson's *Color Experiment No. 15* (2010), provides an experience of dynamic color through space at the apex of the hallway off the master suite. Roy Lichtenstein's 1994 *Nude with Blue Hair* is displayed on the left-facing wall.

The dining room furniture in this corner, with its incomparable views, is from the Italian company Giorgetti. The extending maple table leaves fit into the thin steel base for storage. The chairs are upholstered in saddle leather. Both table and seating elements were chosen for their low profile and discreet presence so nothing competes with the city views.

The furniture also works as a complement to the architecture. As the night reveals its brilliance, the table melts into the dark floor, and the chairs become partners to the white window mullions.

140

Mark Bradford's *Kryptonite* (2006) is a mixed media collage with
billboard paper installed directly onto the wall. Upside-down figures
by Georg Baselitz (*Dix*, 2008) are installed in tandem with Ed Ruscha's
blue *Quality Other* (1982) in the entry. OPPOSITE: Wendell Castle's
Lap Dog (2008) table sits in the study overlooking all of Central Park.

The living room meets the study, in a remarkable confluence of fine and applied art. Along with the Baselitz, there is Yves Klein's *Table d'Or* (1961), made of three thousand sheets of gold leaf encased in Plexiglas; an anthropomorphic rope-wrapped chair by Christian Astuguevieille; and James Rosenquist's *Star Thief* (1979). Here, as elsewhere throughout the apartment, white walls, lacquered millwork, ebonized floor, and neutral-toned suede sofas deliberately keep the palette as quiet as possible to allow the collection its full expression.

In the breakfast room, which sits at the hinge between the kitchen and the more formal dining area, the industrial quality of the metal-and-lacquer *Yacht Table* from Soane Britain pairs well with three expressionistic photographs by Robert Mapplethorpe of the bodybuilder Lisa Lyon from 1981 to 1982. Though it's not visible in the picture, the entire banquette is open to an east-southeastern view that stretches all the way past the great bridges spanning the East River, beyond the Narrows to the Atlantic Ocean.

146

The languid, luxuriant quality of Tom Wesselmann's 1996 *Monica* expresses perfectly the mood of the open and airy master bedroom. We designed all of the built-in furnishings, including the white lacquer bed, which features an ultra-thin television that rises from the footboard and pivots 360 degrees. Reading lights are discreetly tucked behind the headboard. The egg-shaped ambient lights create even illumination that flows into the abundant natural light. As in the living room, the neutral palette—gray suede on the furniture, a similarly toned handwoven leather, linen, and fishing-line headboard—avoids competition with the spectacular views of Central Park.

ABOVE: Anselm Kiefer's beautifully textured and toned *Adam and Lilith* (2009), a gouache on photographic paper, hangs in the guest suite.
OPPOSITE: Entering the foyer, one's eyes fall first on the view, then travel to the right—arriving at Antony Gormley's 2007 *Standing Matter V*, a spectacular anchor for an exceptional collection.

A PASSION
FOR PORTRAITURE

"Portraits convey a wider truth
about the individual's relationship
to the world."

—PAUL MOORHOUSE, CURATOR,
20TH CENTURY, NATIONAL PORTRAIT GALLERY, LONDON

ESIGNING A VERY BIG HOUSE—EVEN ONE AS HANDSOME AS THIS
15,000-square-foot (1,394-square-meter), four-story residence in the Lincoln Park district of
Chicago—involves a special challenge. A structure of this size runs the risk of seeming cold and
intimidating, precisely the opposite of the enveloping and welcoming mood my clients sought.
They also wanted their home to accommodate the very different and specific needs, relating to
sports, work, and travel, of the family's members.

We first addressed the architectural material palette—which, as the project was initiated by
a developer who marketed residences with preexisting amenities packages, ran the risk of making
the home look like every other traditional Lincoln Park home. In this instance, my clients chose
to enhance the package to make their home more personal, so we designed the interiors prior to
the start of construction, producing a bespoke framework reflective of the couple's desire for a
familial environment that drew together influences from eastern and European cultures.

One of the major departures from a typical residential design involved the choice of French
limestone for the floors. While limestone might seem an odd selection for an interior that needed
warming up, we counterbalanced the stone with dark, rich walnut doors, library beams and
bookshelves, and the application of walnut liners to the elegant archways. The balance between
the materials enabled us to create an original interior that was both inviting to inhabit and endowed
with intriguing cultural references.

We also personalized the house by introducing an artistic narrative that grew out of the
wife's attraction to portraiture. I'd been wrestling with how to address the many elevations and
the complete absence of art, and began by exposing my client to different kinds of subject matter
in etchings and lithographs. After she bypassed the landscapes and still lifes, I discovered that she
was fascinated by faces and what they reveal about individuals' inner lives. Her fascination made

A series of drawings, etchings, and lithographs by Matisse, Bissière, and Toulouse-Lautrec—all
of them portraits made in the 1920s, and with stylistic elements common to the period—
line the stairway wall in this Lincoln Park residence. They strike an intimate moment in this
four-story, 15,000-square-foot (1,394-square-meter) home. The bust of Shiva is from Indonesia.

The graceful pair of Joseph Piccillo charcoal drawings, Candida Höfer's bravura photograph on the dining room wall, and the Robert Polidori peeking out from beneath the stair attest to our client's love of portraiture and personality. Despite the great expanse of French limestone floor, the space is warmed up by the dark, rich walnut lining the archways and openings and making its way up the Georgian-style stair. The balance of architectural materials is as important to the success of the design as the art and furnishings.

perfect sense, as she's a psychologist. We put together a collection supported by portraits by such masters as Matisse, Toulouse-Lautrec, and Mary Cassatt, drawings and etchings of historic significance. To this we added contemporary artworks connected to personal themes—charcoal drawings of dancers by Joseph Piccillo that capture the psychological underpinnings of movement, and a wall-size Candida Höfer photograph of a library in Portugal that speaks to my clients' love of education and reading.

Because an important part of my design approach involves thinking about how people like to live—and understanding how they might find joy in the ways their environment represents them to others—we worked hard to make sure the plan fit with the family's needs. We included accommodations for public functions, such as a double kitchen that remains partially closed off—so that heavy preparation can take place out of view—as well as more personal amenities, among them the multiple circulation routes through the master bedroom, bath, closets, and office area (which enable the couple to bathe, dress, work, travel, and sleep without disrupting each other's very different routines).

The house expresses the importance, in our profession, of establishing trust. If the interior is a portrait of its inhabitants, it is no less a portrait of a designer-client relationship founded on respect, understanding, and the ability to listen.

The dining room seems to expand into the photograph of an eighteenth-century academic library in Portugal, deepening and dramatizing the space. A chandelier that could easily belong to the world of the image strengthens the expansive effect. The three Boston & Sandwich candlesticks seem entirely at home with the Venetian glass.

Two 1949 Henry Moore collographs—study maquettes for sculptures—hang above matching vitrines in the dining room. The mirrored table—unlike a wooden version, which would have made the space feel like any other dining room—simultaneously disappears and brings the environment to life, reflecting the light and capturing the animation of lively communal space. We upholstered the walls in a silk with a python-skin weave pattern: Apart from the luxuriant quality the silk imparts, it dampens sound in a room with stone floors and no carpet (a preference for every dining room).

A Robert Polidori photograph in the back corridor leading to the garden(ABOVE), and the Vic Muniz photograph, visible from the front door in the entry corridor (OPPOSITE), achieve different effects. The Polidori extends and ennobles what is essentially a functional space. The hypnotic Muniz draws visitors forward into the grand stair hall.

There is no art in the library, yet its many moments collectively comprise a pointillist tableau as rich as any canvas. The cinnabar vessel on the table, the yellow Peking glass, and the Tibetan chests on either side of the fireplace are favorite objects. The eglomise mirror is precisely the same as the one opposite it—more than forty feet (12 meters) away—in the living room (which also has an identical spherical chandelier). The effect is similar to that of a mirrored grand ballroom, in which reflections are repeated into infinity. The walnut beams reinforce the room's warmth and human scale, and the decorative details add an overlay of quiet narrative.

The carpet in the master bedroom, one of our tone-on-tone patterns, serves to unite what is, in fact, a very large room. The carved wood Anglo-Indian bed anchors the center of the tripartite layout. A chaise longue at one end offers a private place to relax and read, and a sitting area in front of the fireplace (not seen) provides an opportunity for shared contemplation. We selected the chinoiserie Georgian secretary for its great beauty—and also because it can contain a large television (which mercifully disappears when the doors are closed).

The entrance to the master suite (ABOVE) features a gilt-framed
David Kroll canvas above a table showcasing an Ani Kasten bowl.
On the other side of the central stair hall and on the opposite side
of the house, carved Southeast Asian gates (OPPOSITE), illuminated
by mother-of-pearl lanterns, guard the children's bedrooms.

A Chinese-red lacquered island delightfully anchors the kitchen and adjacent informal dining area, which in turn is open to the family room. The stone-base table seems to grow up directly out of the French limestone floor. Beneath the cabinets on either side of the stove are sliding doors that open up to a second prep kitchen, which remains largely concealed from view. The least utilitarian end, which contains the handsome bar, is also the most visible. Once again, walnut—in this case, on the ceiling—brings warmth and casualness to a large, potentially overwhelming space.

170

COUTURE BY DESIGN

"Art washes away from the
soul the dust of everyday life."
—PABLO PICASSO

WHEN A CLIENT HAS A GREAT SENSE OF PERSONAL STYLE (one reflected in her appreciation of and taste for haute couture), a thoughtfully selected portfolio of superb classic and contemporary furniture, and an art collection that includes such present-day masters as Glenn Ligon, Maren Hassinger, Julie Mehretu, and Greg Lauren, a designer's task becomes one of editing, curation, and, crucially, capturing a tone. In this instance, the required tone was one of urbanity expressed as a spare modern elegance, with an overlay of muted glamour that could, on the one hand, dazzle a living room filled with guests and, on the other, act as a restorative private tonic.

Seeking an ideal distillation of our client's sensibilities—one that would enable us to set the stage in an apartment that required virtually no architectural intervention—we introduced two works by the contemporary Korean artist Keysook Geum. Her remarkable "web" dresses—sculptural objects that capture the fluid beauty of fashion and the female form using paper-coated, interlocking wire webs that suggest the pulse-quick connectivity of the Internet—seemed to synthesize my client's complexity as a connoisseur of fashion, informed collector of art, and formidable businesswoman.

Essential to the design were sumptuousness and sophistication. Thus, the club chair by the fire is upholstered in crocodile, goatskin shades are paired with Parisian artist Ingrid Donat's cast-bronze lamps on either side of the fireplace, and an antelope-skin throw drapes the elegant suede Barcelona chaise that bridges the living and dining areas. The antique garden rug from Doris Leslie Blau, in shades of gray, cool blue, and taupe, combines symmetry with ornament. As the apartment has only a modest amount of furniture, we paid special attention to details that would suggest the use of each of its zones. In the dining area, for example, a table skirt makes the space

A 2005 "web" dress by the contemporary Korean artist Keysook Geum, made from red paper–wrapped wire and coral, captures the sophistication of this high-floor Chicago pied-à-terre—and of our fashion-forward client.

A walnut counter in the kitchen serves as an informal dining and desk space. OPPOSITE: The entry foyer suggests a crystalline elegance. On the Christian Astuguevieille console table, sterling Georg Jensen two-light candelabra designed by Johan Rohde flank a commanding oil-on-handmade-paper nude by Greg Lauren. In this apartment there are no unconsidered choices, and no objects or artworks that lack the strength to stand on their own—including the African ceremonial stool.

less of a pass-through between the living room and kitchen and more a library of sorts, a space one might stop to make a journal entry or read a book. Glenn Ligon's text-on-canvas artwork and the integration of two different types of chairs for lounging and reading reflect this library spirit.

ARTWORKS SUPPORT THE DESIGN'S SPIRIT. In the foyer, a commanding oil-on-handmade-paper nude by Greg Lauren establishes our client's confident taste. Norman Lewis's simple, muted *Procession in White*, over the mantelpiece, encourages conversation or contemplation in the living room. Maren Hassinger's abstract gold and silver lithographs, in the entry to the master suite, serve as an effective introduction to a quiet, fully upholstered retreat.

Our client is a woman who knows what she likes, and to help her translate those desires into this residence has been a supreme honor—not to mention a great professional challenge. And an education: Even the most experienced designer can learn from a client who combines a sophisticated eye with flair and imagination.

Keysook Geum's web sculpture is an elegant dress with a shawl collar—entirely appropriate to the overall glamour and sophistication of the apartment. Similarly sophisticated, the tablecloth is a lovely piece of silk with embroidered patterns. In a relatively small apartment, all spaces must be habitable. In this dining space—essentially a pass-through zone between the kitchen and living room—Glenn Ligon's text-based artwork establishes the tone for an eating area that also serves as a library. The chairs—two different pairs, all very comfortable—can easily be pulled over to become extra living room seating when there's a gathering.

Just as all the objects in the apartment have been thoughtfully selected to contribute to the strongly stated sophistication of the design, its materiality is no less individualized: crocodile skin on the club chair, an antelope-fur throw and pillows, silk velvet on the sofa, pleated goatskin shades on the Ingrid Donat lamps flanking the fireplace, suede upholstery on the Mies van der Rohe chaise. Mounted tortoise shells, on the right-hand side of the fireplace, are grouped beneath Norman Lewis's enigmatic canvas *Procession in White*.

182

ABOVE: Aquired from Doris Leslie Blau, the antique garden
rug is especially fantastic. Such a rug typically suggests
the vegetation and plan of a garden, but this rug's design
also includes a graphic expression of water.

ABOVE: Our client's devotion to the art of fashion is evident in the fabulous dressing closet—in which every pair of shoes inhabits its own vitrine. OPPOSITE: Greg Lauren's softly expressive work on paper reinforces the serenity of the bedroom, in which neutral tones, silk-and-linen damask-upholstered walls, and a surfeit of pillows creates the coziest and most soothing of feminine retreats.

AMERICAN WHIMSY

"The ornament of a house
is the friends who frequent it."
—RALPH WALDO EMERSON

FORT SHERIDAN HAS THE DISTINCTION OF BEING THE FIRST MILITARY INSTALLATION
of its type established by Congress in the Midwest. Interestingly, the fort owed its existence not
to threats posed by foreign enemies or Native Americans but to the need to protect Chicago's
commercial interests from labor unrest (which became especially acute following the 1886
Haymarket Riot). In response to the unrest, the city's elite donated more than six hundred
acres of land, on high bluffs overlooking Lake Michigan, between the communities of Highland
Park and Lake Forest—where the fanciest Chicago families maintained summer homes—and the
first troops arrived in 1887. Whatever the motivation, Fort Sheridan's creation produced superb
architecture. Between 1889 and 1910, sixty-four of the more than ninety buildings erected in
what is now a protected historic district were designed by the firm Holabird & Roche, creators
of Chicago's magnificent Marquette Building. All were constructed from bricks made from clay
extracted from those same bluffs.

After the fort closed in 1993, it received another distinction, becoming the first base to be
sold to a private developer. Ninety-one historic properties were converted into modern homes.
One of the handsomest is this 1890 Queen Anne–style general's quarters, once designated
"Building 9," an imposing structure with a huge lawn that extends all the way to the bluff.

Though the house had been subdivided into multiple residences for several military families
to share, the architects' original intentions were easily perceived, and we set about creating a
contemporary plan that honored the structure's history. We expanded and updated the bathrooms
that connected the master suite to the grand terrace overlooking the lake, and arranged the
children's and guest rooms to maximize privacy. Play spaces of various sorts nested comfortably

In the stair hall of this landmark Holabird & Roche–designed
former general's house hangs a c. 1930s "American Flag"
quilt with an improvised design, one of a diverse collection of
folk art and craft that we displayed around the residence.

A cornucopia of delightful American crafts stands at the front staircase: a pair of painted wooden fish, a carved Uncle Sam figure handpainted by artist Kent Gutzmer, and a new hooked circular rug. Beyond, the design elements are more international. A Chinese lantern stands next to a window seat and pillows covered in antique French tickings. The hand-blocked William Morris wall covering, *Marigold* (1875), is set against the high wainscoting, which originally appeared only in the entryway; we continued it throughout the house to create a strong architectural profile.

beneath the eaves, behind the three windows at the peak of the facade. In the military architectural language of the day, the three windows signified the home of a general. We extended certain of the architectural details, notably the high millwork wainscoting in the entry and the delicate picture rail, throughout the house to create stylistic consistency. And while the original structure was quite substantial, it lacked the kind of casual room in which a young family can relax. In compensation, our team designed an addition to the residence's rear—an architecturally appropriate pavilion with a great room above and a garage below, connected to the main house via a glass breezeway. We united old and new with a long, visually unobstructed axis running from the original front door to the addition's grand stair.

WHILE WE BROUGHT BACK the stateliness of the original architecture, we also made important artistic and decorative contributions. Its inherent formality notwithstanding, the house's contemporary function as a casual, away-from-the-city second home—an inviting getaway in which family and friends can relax—required that we introduce warmth and whimsy into the whole environment, both inside and out. So we began to build a collection of simple folk art: weather vanes in two and three dimensions, penny-pitch game boards, a comical wooden airplane by Ed Larson with passengers that bob up and down as the propeller turns, hand-fashioned road signs from produce stands. We also put together a selection of colorful, vividly patterned antique quilts: an artful interpretation of the American flag in the living room, a velvet Victorian crazy quilt in the master suite, and a Triple Irish Chain in the library, among others. These were suspended from the picture rails on ten-foot-high (3-meter-high) walls. Everything remains touchable, approachable, lighthearted—and available for all to enjoy.

The objects, fabrics, and textures, too, promote casualness and comfort. We made extensive use of painted furniture and upholstered or slipcovered sofas and chairs using antique French ticking, old quilts, and patterned textiles. The palette, rich in olive and spring greens, light blue, and russet, draws in the house's natural environs. Furnishings are the opposite of precious.

In the living room, a message of welcome is sent—literally—by the wall-mounted hooked rug from Pennsylvania, c. 1920–40. The handmade trolley—part of an old train set—is a beautifully worked example of the folk art that appears throughout the house. A pair of painted wood-frame antique wicker chairs face the cane-sided Sheraton-style sofa.

The room is brimming with fascinating objects—the mantelpiece alone holds a rooster weather vane, a selection of miniature bowling pins, and a game board—but it works because of the relationships between patterns and forms (which carries over into the textiles as well). For example, the sculptural plant stand in the corner shares its profile with the gingko-patterned stencil on the upper walls. The coffee table was created from a Chinese money chest.

We built the dining room table from reclaimed floorboards, and the gallery showcases rope rugs created by the master weaver Sam Kasten. Like the overall design, applied details, including a gingko-leaf wall pattern, the "checkerboard" stenciled dining room floor, and William Morris two-tone organic wallpaper, speak of the deeper satisfactions of a craft-based rural life without being "country."

Our clients trusted us to create the entire environment, and the result is a well-judged balance between strong-boned interior architecture and the collection's cheerful, beautifully handcrafted objects, artworks, and quilts.

The staircase leading to the new great room is flanked by handsome utilitarian objects, notably the pair of antique Chinese well buckets suspended beneath old wooden shutters. A simple chain-stitched wool runner leads up to the superb "prancing horse" weather vane that waits at the top of the stairs. All the many craft objects reinforce the house's history and its spirited, unpretentious mood.

ABOVE: Three discreet Karl Blossfeldt photographs—part of a much larger collection of Blossfeldts in the stair hall—float quietly opposite a colorful Double Irish Chain quilt in the library. In a space that has the flavor of a North African salon, the cornstalk lamp adds American-style whimsy. OPPOSITE: In the dining room, a penny-pitch board hangs above a one-of-a-kind hand-carved whirligig by Ed Larson. The yellow cabinet against the white wainscot represents a clean transition from architecture to furniture.

The three windows directly below the front gable signified that this was the residence of a general. The house stands 150 yards (137 meters) from the edge of the bluff overlooking Lake Michigan. In the sun porch/breakfast room, the Chinese parrots enjoy the same lake view. Antique French ticking on the banquette is paired with an American crewelwork tablecloth and Italian spongeware.

A Victorian crazy quilt hangs above an Anglo-Indian bed in the master suite. A pair of superb antique wicker chairs sits beneath topiary plants in the narrow windows. Lamps made from seltzer bottles command the night tables. In the adjoining sitting room (OPPOSITE), the Star of Bethlehem quilt is a standout, and the down-filled sofa is of a rare level of comfort—perfect for napping.

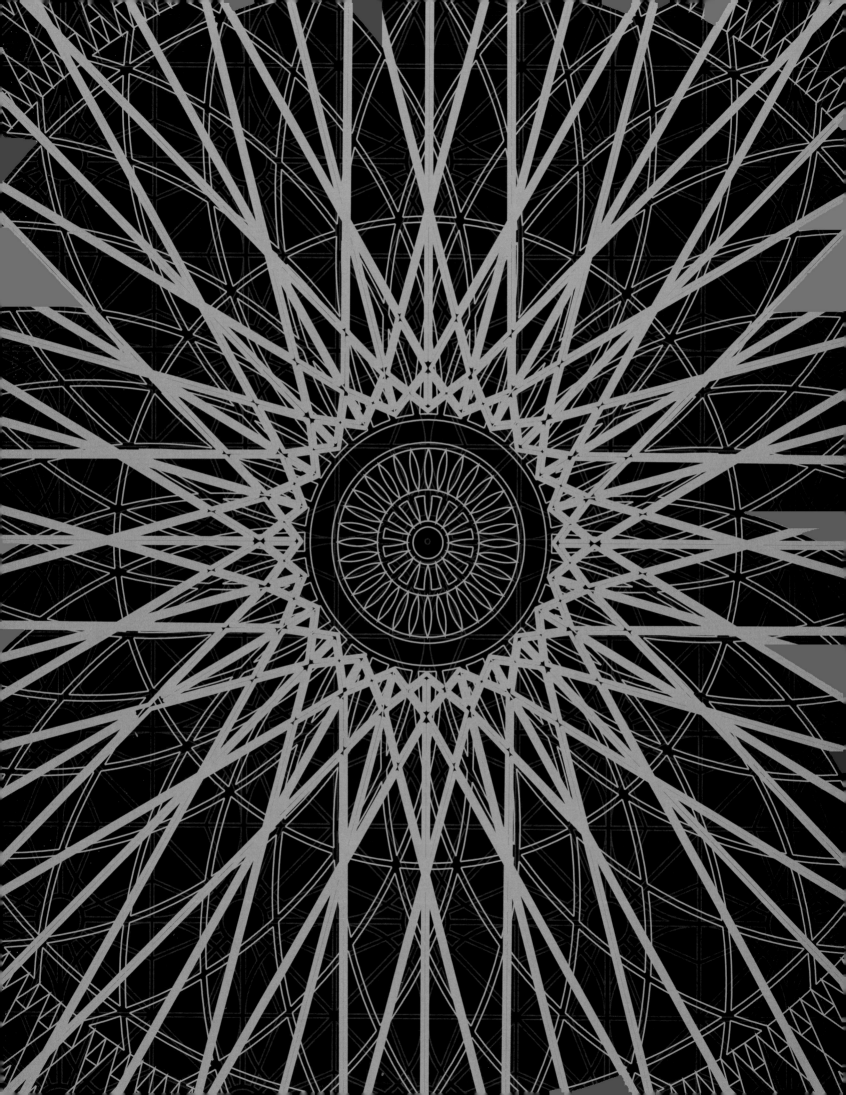

SHEDDING LIGHT

"Beauty is the
promise of happiness."
—STENDHAL

"ADAPTIVE REUSE" REFERS TO THE REPURPOSING OF A structure for a function other than the one for which it was originally intended. What this somewhat dry term doesn't capture is the high drama that can result when the latent promise of a utilitarian building is coaxed forth through the application of design. It's the kind of challenge we'd always wanted to undertake—and with the firm's second project at Fort Sheridan, we were given the opportunity.

The army-designated Building 89 had all of the magisterial elegance of so many of the Holabird & Roche buildings at the former military garrison. It was an artillery shed, with sixteen 10-by-10-foot (3-by-3-meter) Romanesque archways—eight on each of the building's long sides—through which horses would pull out the ammo-loaded caissons. While it was run-down and surrounded by yards of blacktop, excitement about the building's potential seized us the moment we walked inside. The space was stunning—132 feet (40 meters) long and 32 feet (10 meters) wide, with a ceiling that rose to 25 feet (7.5 meters) at its peak—all entirely unobstructed. Originally the thought had been to create two residences within the 4,200-square-foot (390-square-meter) plan. But standing in the vastness, with rhythmic rows of Romanesque archways on either side of us, we realized the shed's potential as a truly spectacular single-family home.

The challenge was to find a way to add rooms without losing the visceral impact of the unobstructed volume. Ironically, it was my experience designing corporate modernist high-rises that pointed me toward a solution. In office buildings, clear-span space typically surrounds a core containing elevators and climate-control systems—the better to leave the exterior curtain walls, which provide light and views, unobstructed. Accordingly, into the shed we inserted a pair of two-story cores—both rising the full height of the building—one incorporating private spaces

In the living room/entry area in this historic former artillery shed, we inserted a very contemporary steel stair, leading to an openwork steel bridge that permits access to the house's second-story rooms.

and bedrooms, the other holding the dining room, pantry, wine cellar, and exercise room. By contrast, the kitchen and master suite, at either end of the structure, and the living room and entry in the center, were left completely open—soaring full-height spaces that celebrated the voluminous quality of the original architecture. Best of all, as the two cores were set in from the exterior walls, we were able to create a circulation path around the entire perimeter—resulting in two unobstructed 132-foot-long (40-meter-long) promenades, lined with huge arched windows admitting both eastern and western light. Bronze rods running the full length of each promenade carried sheer linen drapery that, when drawn, filled the entire space with a soft and elegant glow.

THE USE OF TWIN CORES CREATED another way to add visual impact to the already dramatic interior. To create access to, and circulation between, the two second-story areas, we set a grand contemporary stairway in the entry, and it rose to a modernist openwork steel-frame bridge, a structure that spanned the living room. A visitor walking in the front door would behold the vast, loft-like space, with a massive fireplace on one side, the stair on the other, and the bridge high above—a remarkable sight.

For the floor, we selected wide-board sculpted and beveled "character" hickory, with butterfly ties inserted, as though the original flooring had been preserved and repaired. To create architectural continuity between the inside and outside of the residence, we used reclaimed brick from elsewhere in the fort to replicate the archways' exterior surround detail on the interior. We chose to replace the sixteen original, partially wooden doors with fully glazed versions, but used the originals to clad a newly added garage.

When Building 89's transformation from abandoned shed to gracious home was complete, the project received a Chicago Landmarks Preservation Award—a lovely accolade for a project that had already provided so much joy.

The scale of the 27-foot-high (8-meter-high) room can be gauged by the chandelier's diameter: six feet (2 meters). The decorative star on the new cold-rolled-steel fireplace is taken from one of the tie rods that held the original building together. A superb Calder stabile sits atop a Chinese trunk, and a Tibetan bed serves as a coffee table. FOLLOWING PAGES: LEFT: We inserted mirrored panes into a pair of the original doors opposite the bar to "extend" the space. RIGHT: We added the interior brick arch surrounds to bring the structure's architectural detailing inside.

To reinforce the rhythm created by the arches—and to break up the massive scale of the continuous rooms—we turned the boards of the sculpted and beveled-edge "character" hickory floors at each arch, setting them precisely perpendicular to the doors' center points. The simple, translucent draperies, suspended from shepherd's hooks, are easily pulled together to mute the strong eastern and western light. On the Tibetan chest in the dining room, the vessel on the right is by Picasso, as is the intriguing double-sided pastel hanging above it. The bookshelves in the master bedroom are visible at the far end of the hall.

216

The antique Irish butcher-block table is one of several elements we used to bring character to the expansive kitchen. OPPOSITE: We added a sunken reading pit under a portion of the twelve-by-thirty-foot (3.7-by-9-meter) arbor, so that on stepping out of the living room into the garden, one has a pleasing sense of being "held" while in the vast space.

In the master bedroom, one of a pair of Chinese demilune tables, positioned in front of the archway, exemplifies how satisfying the interplay between architecture and furniture can be. The other table is on the room's opposite side. In a house with an abundance of art, some of the most interesting pieces can be found in this room. They range in spirit from Joseph Piccillo's slightly surreal *Random Notes* over the bed—which includes the film actress Clara Bow, a B-52 bomber, and a raven among its many curiosities—to an etching, on the night table, by the great cartoonist Bill Mauldin. Made shortly after President Kennedy's assassination, it shows Lincoln at the Lincoln Memorial, cradling his head in his hands.

220

JAPANESE BOX

"The noblest pleasure
is the joy of understanding."
—LEONARDO DA VINCI

I
T IS A DESIGN PROBLEM AS OLD AS THE PROFESSION: WHAT TO DO WHEN ONE member of a couple has contemporary, even iconoclastic, tastes while the other hews more closely to the traditional. Our clients were a recently married pair creating a home that could accommodate the peregrinations of several grown-up children in a sprawling, 15,000-square-foot (1,394-square-meter) structure. The husband had an especially sophisticated, world-class art collection, including work by Toulouse-Lautrec and Miró, and objects reflecting his extensive knowledge of Japanese miniature lacquerware. As a busy philanthropist, the wife's primary interest lay in the spaces themselves: developing classic environments that would facilitate evenings of entertaining. What both sensibilities shared was a focus on moments: one visual, the other social. With this in mind, we designed a series of vignettes that combined artworks and objects in tableaux and set them in rooms that frankly celebrated beauty and—whether enjoyed by family, friends, or social-occasion guests—would feel reassuring and traditionally welcoming.

The husband's extensive knowledge of eastern culture led us (along with architect Tony Grunsfeld) to envision the house as a Japanese box divided into elegantly rendered, intercommunicative compartments that collectively formed a narrative. With reclaimed wide-board maple floors and cedar ceilings, we warmed up the existing modernist design of the house.

Having crafted our Japanese box, we then worked room by room. My clients wanted the long entry hall to express an urbane formality suggestive of Park Avenue, which we established with a carved and painted antique Roman desk, directly opposite the front door. At the same

An exceptionally rare black basalt ware "Pegasus" vase from Wedgwood, c. 1800, stands atop a carved Italian console in the entry, flanked by nineteenth-century French candlesticks. Beneath, the aptly named *A Monumental Vessel,* by Per Weiss. FOLLOWING PAGES: LEFT: The Chinese export cabinet and its English base, both from the mid-eighteenth century, are from the Potter Palmer estate. RIGHT: The Gao Brothers' *Miss Mao,* in fiberglass and paint, in the entry hall.

time, we invoked history in a chinoiserie cabinet that had belonged to the Chicago tycoon Potter Palmer.

The living room posed a different set of challenges. It was a very large space, in which even a substantial gathering of people could easily feel overwhelmed. We divided it into three distinct seating areas, all open to one another—good for entertaining, equally comfortable for sitting in solitude. The room showcases a number of precious objects—nineteenth-century wrought-iron-and-tin Spanish Colonial decorative eagle figures, and modern classics such as Ingrid Donat's sculptural armchairs—in a cool, contemporary space, an environment that needed to feel cozy and not too precious to be used. Richly colored upholstery and handcrafted textiles, notably the asymmetrically patterned Moroccan "Great White" rug that spans its center, warm the space. And, given the husband's collection of Japanese miniature laquerware, it was a triumph for us to persuade him to purchase the magnificent pair of imperial Chinese lacquerwork trunks from the Qing Dynasty.

PERHAPS THE MOST COMPLICATED SPACE to create was the dining room, structured around an extraordinary circular Sri Lankan table dating from the seventeenth century and incorporating nearly forty varieties of local wood. We designed two sideboards, handbuilt in the studio of contemporary master craftsman Frank Pollaro. Each incorporates more than 1,600 pieces of ebony and ivory inlay. I came upon four curvaceous low-backed Regency chairs that perfectly complemented the table and created eight more to go with them.

When our client pined for a chandelier, we pointed out that the architecture was too contemporary—and when she insisted, we suggested that only an organic, Dale Chihuly–style construction could work. The result: an opalescent, specially commissioned Chihuly fixture

The Gene Summers andirons express the same sort of whimsy as the Calder hanging above them. The andiron and the foo dog on the corner of the ceramic capital base seem to be conversing, a chat observed from above by the four cast-bronze women on Ingrid Donat's armchair. (Donat also stitched and handpainted the chair fabric.) The rug is a Moroccan "Great White."

The challenge posed by the overscaled living room was resolved by dividing it
into three zones: a more casual relaxing area (above, in the foreground);
a formal space in the center, defined by the fireplace and carpet; and, by the piano,
a cozy place for a tête-à-tête or a game of chess. Two sets of eagles—Indian
behind the sofa, Spanish by the colorful abstract canvas—stand guard.

From the vantage point of the fireplace, the carpet becomes an allée leading to the garden, which communicates freely with the living room when the sliding glass doors are open. (The residence, which was enlarged five times, here reveals its origins as a humble pool house.) The juxtaposition of living room and garden is striking: Because the living room's center and the garden both convey different kinds of formal design, the rooms are, in a way, echoes of each other. The pair of Chinese chests facing each other feature exquisitely lacquered interiors.

The American elm millwork wall in the den serves as an appropriately elegant backdrop for a superb grouping of vintage George Hurrell movie-star glamour photographs, which our client's father collected. The pool table features a custom-designed cowhide cover, which we created to give the room (which is used as much for entertaining as for pool) greater flexibility via a contemporary twist. The challenge of putting the cover together—expressing the edges one finds on a single hide on a larger scale—proved especially intriguing.

236

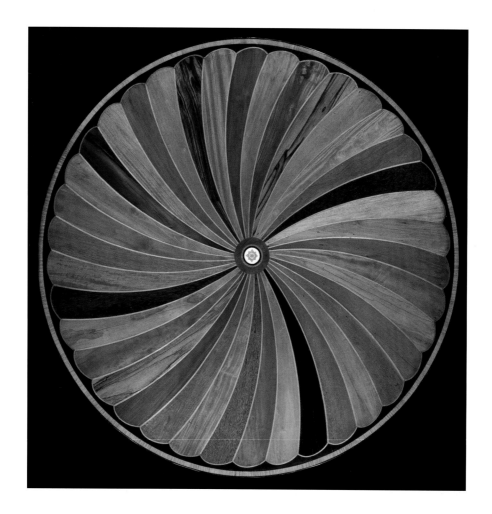

inspired by a small gem of a painting, by John Singer Sargent, of an octopus. The fixture required the complete reconstruction of the new wood ceiling to install. I had lobbied tirelessly to keep the husband's collection of Miró aquatints together in the space—"Think 'oceanic,'" I said. In the end, that mantra proved truer than anticipated.

Strong-minded clients who are passionate and brilliant are a designer's dream. It is always a pleasure to have a blank canvas, but it is even better to have one's ideas put to the test, and to find ways to bring together competing desires without compromise.

OPPOSITE: Frank Pollaro's sideboard, based on our original design, features 1,600 slivers of ebony and ivory; on top, a moss-filled Jeff Koons puppy keeps an eye on a sterling Buccellati "lobster" casserole. "Butterfly" boxes—featuring real insects "fluttering" around a painted backdrop—are early-twentieth-century American. PREVIOUS PAGES: Dale Chihuly's "octopus" chandelier writhes above a seventeenth-century Sri Lankan table pictured above.